Water
as a Liquid

by Helen Frost

Consulting Editor: Gail Saunders-Smith, Ph.D.

Reviewer: Carolyn M. Tucker
Water Education Specialist
California Department of Water Resources

Pebble Books

an imprint of Capstone Press
Mankato, Minnesota

Pebble Books are published by Capstone Press
818 North Willow Street, Mankato, Minnesota 56001
http://www.capstone-press.com

Library of Congress Cataloging-in-Publication Data
Frost, Helen, 1949–
       Water as a liquid/by Helen Frost.
       p. cm.—(Water)
       Includes bibliographical references and index.
       Summary: Simple text presents facts about water in its liquid state, where it is
found, and some of its properties.
       ISBN 0-7368-0410-2
       1. Water—Juvenile literature. [1. Water.] I. Title. II. Series: Frost, Helen,
1949–   Water.
GB662.3.F76   2000
551.46—dc21   99-19589
                                                                                                        CIP

Note to Parents and Teachers

The Water series supports national science standards for
understanding the properties of water. This book describes and
illustrates water as a liquid. The photographs support early readers
in understanding the text. This book introduces early readers to
subject-specific vocabulary words, which are defined in the Words
to Know section. Early readers may need assistance to read some
words and to use the Table of Contents, Words to Know, Read
More, Internet Sites, and Index/Word List sections of the book.

Table of Contents

Water can be a solid, a gas, or a liquid. Water is a liquid when it is not too cold or too warm.

Water as a liquid
does not have a shape.
It is the shape of
whatever holds it.

Clouds are dust and
tiny drops of water.
Sometimes the water falls
to the ground as rain.

Some water goes into the ground. People pump groundwater from wells.

Some water fills
lakes and rivers.

Water flows from high places to low places. Rivers carry water to oceans.

Most water on the earth is in oceans. Water in oceans is salt water. Salt water is not safe for people to drink.

Water in most rivers and lakes is freshwater. Freshwater is safe for people to drink.

Water is a part of all
living things. People,
plants, and animals
need water to live.

Words to Know

freshwater—water without salt in it; water from the faucet is freshwater.

groundwater—water that is found underground; groundwater can be pumped from wells.

liquid—a substance that flows freely; a liquid does not have a shape; water is a liquid between 32 degrees Fahrenheit and 212 degrees Fahrenheit (0 degree Celsius and 100 degrees Celsius).

ocean—a very large body of water; most water on the earth is in oceans.

pump—to force a liquid from one place into another place using a machine

salt water—water with a lot of salt in it; water in oceans is salt water; salt water is not safe for people to drink.

well—a deep hole in the ground out of which people pump water

Read More

Davies, Kay and Wendy Oldfield. *Rain.* See for Yourself. Austin, Texas: Raintree Steck-Vaughn, 1996.

Morris, Neil. *Rivers and Lakes.* The Wonders of Our World. New York: Crabtree Publishing, 1998.

Saunders-Smith, Gail. *Rain.* Weather. Mankato, Minn: Pebble Books, 1998.

Wick, Walter. *A Drop of Water: A Book of Science and Wonder.* New York: Scholastic, 1997.

Internet Sites

Freshwater
http://www.mobot.org/MBGnet/fresh/index.htm

Kids' Stuff
http://www.epa.gov/ogwdw/kids

Water Facts of Life
http://www.awwa.org/waterfac.htm

Water Science for Schools
http://wwwga.usgs.gov/edu

Index/Word List

animals, 21
clouds, 9
drink, 17, 19
dust, 9
earth, 17
freshwater, 19
gas, 5
ground, 9, 11

groundwater, 11
lakes, 13, 19
liquid, 5, 7
live, 21
need, 21
oceans, 15, 17
people, 11, 17,
   19, 21

plants, 21
rain, 9
rivers, 13, 15, 19
safe, 17, 19
salt water, 17
solid, 5
wells, 11

Word Count: 141
Early-Intervention Level: 10

Editorial Credits
Mari C. Schuh, editor; Timothy Halldin, cover designer; Kimberly Danger,
   photo researcher

Photo Credits
Cheryl A. Ertelt, 14
ColePhoto/Robin Cole, 10
David F. Clobes, 18
Index Stock Imagery/Carmen Northern (1989), 16
International Stock/Art Brewer, cover
James P. Rowan, 8
John Elk III, 4
Photri-Microstock/Novastock, 6
Richard Hamilton Smith, 12
Robert McCaw, 1, 20

Special thanks to science teacher Mike Lundgren of Fairmont High School in
Fairmont, Minnesota, for his helpful assistance with this book.